Leadership
secrets
The experts tell all!

About the author
Michael Heath is Managing Director of Michael Heath Consulting, a Learning and Development Consultancy established in 1999. Drawing upon nearly 20 years' experience of working with an impressive portfolio of international organizations, he offers a wealth of practical knowledge and insights to address the challenges that leaders face. He is the author of *Management*, also in the **business secrets** series.

Leadership
secrets

Collins
A division of HarperCollins*Publishers*
1 London Bridge Street, London SE1 9GF

www.BusinessSecrets.net

First published in Great Britain in 2010 by HarperCollins*Publishers*
Published in Canada by HarperCollins*Canada*. www.harpercollins.ca
Published in Australia by HarperCollins*Australia*. www.harpercollins.com.au
Published in India by HarperCollins*PublishersIndia*. www.harpercollins.co.in

A catalogue record for this book is available from the British Library.

ISBN 978-0-00-732805-5

Contents

A memorable leader – for the right reasons!

Over the last 50 years there have been over 1,000 studies to establish what leadership is. How leaders behave. What traits they have. I don't have much time for them, and nor should you. Instead I've filled this book with the convictions, skills, beliefs and techniques that great leaders need. The behaviours you see great leaders demonstrating every day.

And what experience am I drawing on? It's not only the 20 years or so I've been working in the world of leaders as a consultant. But all the other years when I experienced leadership first hand, as a corporate employee. I've been around leaders it was a privilege to know and leaders it was dangerous to know. Both extremes – and all the leaders in-between – provided me with insights into what really great leadership is.

So I've done all of the research for you. If you're a leader or an aspiring leader, then let us spend some time together. I want you to be a memorable leader – for all of the right reasons! And I'm willing to share my 50 **secrets** of leadership with you. These **secrets** are spread over seven chapters:

■ Leadership character. There is a core of behaviours, values and characteristics that great leaders have. They're the backbone that makes them the strong, principled individuals that people look up to.

■ Leadership responsibilities. Leaders change things. Their responsibilities are to take what they see and reshape it to meet the demands of the world tomorrow.

■ Leadership strategy. The ability to set a strategic direction is where leaders thrive – or fall. But strategy is much more than the 'where', it's also the 'how' and the 'why'.

■ Leadership and execution. It's the plain old 'getting it done'. It's so easy to 'talk the talk'. But execution is about getting everyone to 'walk the walk'.

■ Leadership and change. Change happens. The working world doesn't have a habit of waiting around for others to catch up. But not everyone who works for you is going to think the same…

■ Leadership influence. You need friends. Not so much in high places but in the important places. They need nurturing if you're serious about getting your initiatives off the ground.

■ Leadership and the team. You need great people around you. You also need to repeatedly challenge them to keep them great. They're going to have to pick up the goals and make them their own.

Dip into the book or read it front to back – whichever you prefer. But promise me this. You won't skip the questions I ask of you. These questions help you gain the insights into the skills that will turn you into a truly memorable leader.

Great leaders leave their values in the hearts of those who worked for them.

Leadership character

There are different styles of leadership but all of them depend on character. That's why I've made character the subject of the first chapter of this book. Later chapters deal with practical aspects of leadership, but first and foremost the leader must possess the essential attributes of leadership: courage, patience, a steely mental toughness and the passion and enthusiasm needed to bring about change. Leadership that doesn't demonstrate these principles is spineless.

1.1

Put courage first

Winston Churchill once said, "Courage is rightly considered the foremost of the virtues, for upon it all others depend." Leadership courage often means experiencing emotional or even physical discomfort. Is it the first of the leadership virtues? There have been many instances in history where a failure in leadership was the result of a failure in courage.

When people told Terry Anderson, the US journalist who was held hostage in Lebanon for seven years how courageous he had been, he modestly pointed out, "People are capable of doing an awful lot when they have no choice, and I had no choice. Courage is when you have choices." Leaders are constantly faced by choices and the kind of courage they have to display is often moral and ethical. It is the mark of the leader who stands up for a principle when others would prefer

one minute wonder What one great thing could you achieve if you knew you could not fail? Describe the outcome to yourself. What is it that holds you back from achieving it? Are there too many obstacles? Time? Energy? Or a lack of courage?

"The brave man is not he who does not feel afraid, but he who conquers that fear"

Nelson Mandela, South African political leader

to walk away. It is about acting out of integrity and being true to one's principles. It is the courage of the person who, when they realize that something important is being lost, will take a stand and ask the questions that no one else dare ask.

This bravery, this sense of principle is inspiring to others. It makes its mark in people's hearts. It is a stand for truth and what is believed to be right. Such behaviour sets out clear boundaries and inspires those who feel they are working in ambiguity. When, for whatever reason, a team loses heart then it takes a great leader to make them address their fear. To show that the doubts and fear in the team are the very things holding them back.

A leader who displays this moral courage honours those who also show the same behaviour. It is the beginning of an ethically motivated team. It leads on to ethically motivated departments and even whole organizations.

The moral courage needed to follow your principles and take difficult decisions will inspire your team.

1.2

Be mentally tough

We all have moments in our lives when we come to a difficult situation that screams to us to give in. Everyone else has given up so why don't you? Do you stay and fight? Or do you suddenly feel lonely and join the others walking away? Welcome to the world of mental toughness.

Being a leader calls upon mental toughness many times over. For example, you've communicated the goal to everyone. But now you find that circumstances have changed in a way you could never have foreseen. You still want the goal. But people are telling you to 'get real' and let the goal go.

case study Times were hard and Manish was told he had to make cuts in his management team. The problem was that the manager whose role was least needed happened to be the most popular. When Manish gave Vijay the news he took it badly. He made the remaining weeks of his notice hell for Manish. Many staff refused to talk to Manish. Likewise, peers who

Such moments are lonely. And it's often these moments that highlight just how isolating the position of being a leader is. It's the 'moment of truth': to carry on or give up.

The American football coach Vince Lombardi said of mental toughness: "Its qualities are sacrifice and self-denial. It is combined with a perfectly disciplined will that refuses to give in. It's a state of mind – you could call it character in action."

Mental toughness is about recognizing the fight as a long one. There are times when you have everyone with you. And times you're on your own. Either way, a mentally tough leader will be determined to see it through to achieve what they know is the right outcome.

One person is a great example of this combination of passion and patience: KFC's Colonel Sanders. He experienced 1,009 rejections before the first restaurant agreed to sell his chicken for him!

Mental toughness is the determination to carry on against the odds to achieve success.

liked Vijay also made sure he had a hard time. Then Manish's boss asked if he'd made the right decision! At every turn Manish was doubted. Vijay left. Within weeks he was rarely talked about. Relationships settled back down. Manish had made the right decision and stayed with it. His mental toughness was tested and he triumphed. He is now a director in that company.

1.3

Discipline yourself

Self-discipline is putting aside what you'd like to do to concentrate on something you need to do. It's recognizing the temptations, desires and habits that can seduce you towards an easier path. But a leader calls upon an inner strength that makes them choose the harder – and right – path. And that path involves sacrifice and commitment.

In Greek mythology, Odysseus was warned about the sirens. The sirens sang music so beautiful that it lured sailors to their death on the rocks around their island. To escape, Odysseus made his men plug their ears and tied himself to the mast. Because of this they successfully kept their ship on course.

one minute wonder Which habits could you change by asserting more self-discipline? Write them down. What alternative behaviours would bring better results? What justifications do you give yourself for your negative or unhelpful behaviours? What's the first thing you can do to exert self-discipline and get these habits under control?

Self-discipline is the same choice. If you go with your emotions rather than your inner strength and logic, your purpose or goal may smash upon the rocks. You need to exert will-power over your desires and exercise real self-control. Your self-discipline will be recognized – and often imitated – by those you lead.

So what prevents us from conquering these emotions and choosing the right path? What some do is fool themselves and find justifications for their choices. Why don't I exercise more? I haven't the time! Why don't I get up earlier? I work so hard and get so tired. Why do I drink? If only you knew the stress I'm under!

If we can fool ourselves so easily, are we fit to lead others? If we can't be truthful to ourselves, how truthful are we to those we lead? We need to train ourselves to control our behaviours. Show the strength of our own willpower by refusing to be ruled by weaknesses or habits.

Management consultant Stephen Covey thought that discipline was freedom: "The undisciplined are slaves to moods, appetites and passions". Leadership is about freely choosing thoughts and actions that lead to improvement. It's denying the easy gratifications that surround us and keeping true to our goals. To ask others to demonstrate self-discipline involves us setting the example.

Self-discipline means denying yourself what you want to do and doing what you need to do.

1.4

Value your character

You may think your words count. But they don't count anywhere near as much as your deeds count. Your deeds speak to your team about your character. They convey what you value and who you are. They are your values in action. So you must make sure that your actions are driven by the right values.

Everybody has values. Unfortunately some people's values are unattractive. They value themselves and their own feelings of superiority. They value their own needs being met – even at others' expense. Do you recognize those values? You've probably witnessed them in someone you've worked for. And that's the interesting thing. Even when people try and cover up their negative values, they can't. They leak out. They become visible.

case study When Tony told me how popular he was as a manager, I straight away began to have doubts. Why did he feel the need to tell me? Tony told me other things as well. He said his door was always open to his staff. That his values were respect and putting his employees first. Talking to his staff proved the

"Character is doing what's right when nobody's looking"

J C Watts, US congressman

But positive values leak out as well. These values appear in the way that we behave towards our team. As General Norman Schwarzkopf said, "The main ingredient of good leadership is good character. This is because leadership involves conduct and conduct is determined by values."

We probably have two sets of values. The first values are those that we tell people about. They are our 'declared values'. The other set of values are those that people actually see in action – our 'demonstrated' values. A person who has a strong character is always trying to make sure that their declared values match their demonstrated values.

When the two sets of values match then you have someone who is truly authentic. They possess the right values-driven character. As a leader they make decisions based on these values. And an authentic leader usually makes the right decisions.

Authenticity is when your declared values correspond with your demonstrated values.

opposite. "He hasn't time for anyone," complained one employee. "Always has one eye on his career," said his team leader. Tony was a man who thought that by merely repeating his declared values to people, they would not notice the real values that he had. Real values always become visible.

1.5

Project confidence

Is it possible for a leader always to project confidence? Surely every leader walks into situations which they don't feel confident about. It could be a presentation in front of a large audience. It might be dealing with a very emotional issue. There are many things to throw the leader out of their comfort zone.

Work is always going to put these challenges in our way. The way we deal with them conveys a lot to those around us. So it's vital that we maintain a confident manner. We need to approach difficult or ambiguous situations with the conviction that 'all will come good'. So how can you sustain a belief in one's powers and abilities? Here are some practical techniques to help you appear – and feel – more confident.

1 **Project a positive attitude.** There's a link between our physiological and psychological selves. If we tell ourselves to appear confident, the body assumes the posture of confidence. This begins to make us feel genuinely confident!

2 **Maintain appropriate eye contact.** Every culture has rules about eye contact. In many Western countries, failure to maintain eye contact can be interpreted as submissive.

> "When there is no enemy within, the enemies outside cannot hurt you" **African proverb**

3 **Watch those hands.** Hands are often a big 'give-away' about how someone is feeling. Keep them in control and still. You'll appear much more relaxed.

4 **Prepare thoroughly for any task.** What often drains confidence away is the feeling that we are out of our depth. Preparation reassures us before we go into challenges and is rarely wasted.

5 **Dress confidently.** Going into situations knowing that a shirt or blouse is too tight makes us lose confidence. Dress appropriately and always feel you look smart.

6 **Choose your opinions carefully.** Don't commit to definite opinions that you have trouble defending. Give opinions which you feel confident of defending and do so if challenged.

7 **Notice any feelings of vulnerability.** When people start to feel 'out of their depth' they can feel vulnerable. This vulnerability might express itself in aggressive or submissive behaviour. Stay calm, focused and assertive.

Being able to display confidence, even during difficult periods, gives confidence to the team and keeps morale high.

Good posture and appropriate eye contact project confidence to others.

1.6

Get passionate about your enthusiasm

Enthusiasm and passion are two emotions leaders must possess. And they have to be able to inspire those same qualities in those who surround them. Employees are often swept along by an enthusiastic leader's determination and single-mindedness to realize a goal. In time they too become enthusiastic and passionate about the same things.

What's so different about passion and enthusiasm is that they are not taught but caught. You can't teach people to be passionate or enthusiastic. It's contagious. It spreads like a positive virus through the team. It transforms the energy of people.

I love the origin of the word 'enthusiasm'. It's from the Greek word 'entheos' which translates into 'the God within'. I prefer to think of it as 'the spirit within'. A deep, profound energy that makes you work tirelessly to achieve your goals. So how do we create the right conditions for this magical virus to spread?

"If you aren't fired with enthusiasm, you will be fired with enthusiasm"

Vince Lombardi, American football coach

■ **Maintain an optimistic outlook.** Pessimists and cynics drag everybody down. Face up to all obstacles with the conviction you will succeed.

■ **Find people who share the same passion.** There will be others outside your team who equally share your enthusiasm and passion. Seek them out on bad days!

■ **Control your emotions when faced with disappointment.** When setbacks occur a team might try and read the reactions of the leader. Be aware of this and hide any emotion when confronting setbacks.

■ **Allow people to experience temporary lows.** It's human nature. We all lose enthusiasm occasionally. Just don't let them stay there. Move them quickly to the next tip...

■ **Concentrate on what can be done.** Negative teams meet an obstacle and immediately respond, "Typical. I knew this would happen." You'll only overcome it by concentrating minds on what can be done.

■ **Never let your enthusiasm interfere with your objectivity.** Enthusiasm can, with some people, turn into obsession. Healthy doses of good feedback help you retain that objectivity.

And remember that enthusiasm and passion are not necessarily about bouncing around as if you're on springs all the time. There are many people who are equally enthusiastic but, because they are not as extroverted, will show it in their own way.

Passion is contagious and can spread rapidly through a team.

1.7

Patiently does it

Are you about to rush through this page to get on to the next topic? If so, how much would you really take in? When someone's speaking, are you similarly waiting for them to move on? Being impatient may look dynamic but it rarely has a positive outcome. In fact, impatience often leads to misunderstanding, rework and repair.

■ **Leadership demands patience.** After all, we're taking people not into the next hour, day, week or even month. We're leading them to a distant place. A place that lies over the known horizon. Therefore we must have patience and self-control. So what do we need patience for? We need patience to deal with people, politics and perspective.

■ **Most people are not immovable in their thinking.** But they have to feel that they have control over the decision to change. When pressure is applied they might comply. But they will not be persuaded.

■ **Goals often mean that you will need the assistance of others.** Winning them over to your cause may take time. Thinking that you'll just force it through anyway creates instant enemies. With people, time is a friend – not an enemy.

"Sit by the river long enough... your enemies will float by"

Confucius, Ancient Chinese sage

■ **Every organization has its politics.** You have to read the politics and learn to wait patiently for the right time to move. There are better times to ask people to help you in your goals. Lose patience and you could move too quickly. Worse still, your miscalculation could end that person's good will for ever.

■ **Finally, you must retain perspective.** When it comes to standing your ground for things you really believe in, you want to be sure it's for the right things. Impatient people do not choose their conflicts wisely and suffer as a result. Perspective is also about thinking twice when you're asked to help others. If you're a generous person then you may help. But what you could be doing is sidetracking your team's energies into things that divert them from their goal. Patience involves assessing opportunities and seeing if that's what they really are.

We must patiently take people with us. Take the time to understand the political environment we work in. Retain a cool perspective and make sure that short-term activities really do contribute to our long-term goals.

Impatience can often waste more time, especially having to repair the problems our impatience caused.

1.8

Be a warm touch

We sometimes describe people as 'a really warm person'. We might also refer to someone as being 'cold and distant'. A leader doesn't necessarily have to be liked. But they make life so much easier for themselves when they are. The ability to show genuine personal warmth towards employees can be a real advantage.

Showing personal warmth to people must be genuine. Haven't you noticed that those who only pretend to be personally warm often come across as patronizing and insincere? Insincerity in a leader is usually disastrous. Better to be a cold – but honest – leader than a false, insincere one.

So let's look at those characteristics warm people might possess.

■ **They like people.** They know that everyone has their faults (including themselves!) but they accept people for who they are.

■ **They make the person they're dealing with the centre of attention.** They show strong eye contact and listen carefully to what the other person is saying.

"One kind word can warm three winter months"

Japanese proverb

■ **They take a genuine interest in the lives of others.** They know many people take great pleasure talking about their lives and their families.

■ **They smile and look pleased to see people.** They greet people and show that they are genuinely pleased to see them.

■ **They have open body language.** They appear relaxed and at ease when chatting. They stand in a way that the other person finds comfortable. For example, not standing full on to a shy person.

■ **Their voice has a wide pitch range.** Cold people have a very limited range when speaking. A warm person's wide pitch range conveys real enthusiasm.

■ **They're careful not to dominate the other person.** They make sure that the other person has an equal input to a conversation.

■ **They avoid aggressive behaviour.** Unfortunately, some people start by showing personal warmth but let it turn into the heat of anger!

■ **They care about people.** When someone is upset they quickly look to help. They show empathy with someone who is having a difficult time and listen patiently.

A leader has to be persuasive. And one of the qualities that can aid their ability to persuade is the degree to which they can build and maintain the necessary personal warmth with their team.

People who fake personal warmth can appear insincere and patronizing.

1.9

Develop yourself or get left behind

Early on in my career I remember a saying on the office wall, "When you stop learning, you start dying." Years later I discovered it was by Einstein. A man whose life was a perfect example of continuous self-development. So what is self-development and what can we do to make sure we don't "start dying"?

Self-development is about taking responsibility for our learning. The real benefit is that it keeps our skills relevant – especially in this constantly changing world. It's an appetite that devours new thinking. And if we demonstrate this appetite, our team will also want to eat from that same table.

case study A director I used to work for would often ask me, "Michael, what have you learned lately?" At first I'd be confused. I must have learned something! I'd think back and mumble a few words about a book I'd read or something I'd been told. In time, I got clever and, when I did learn something, would make a mental

So how do we develop ourselves? Try these tips.

■ Take personal responsibility for your own growth. It's not the training team or HR's responsibility. It's yours.
■ Develop a plan that identifies key areas you want to know more about. Keep a learning log where you make notes of important lessons from any book, CD, programme or conversation.
■ Get yourself a mentor. Someone who can facilitate your learning.
■ Broaden your reading. Don't just read the same publications. Go for something that's different. Shake up your thinking.
■ Regularly ask yourself, "What have I learned today?" Don't settle for the obvious. Think about issues in a deeper way.
■ Really listen to someone with whom you're having a disagreement. Ask questions about their point of view. Don't just turn off! You may emerge with a real insight.
■ Tap into other people's experiences. How have they done things? Be a sponge and absorb all of that free education.

Self-development keeps our skills relevant in a constantly evolving workplace.

note to use it when I next saw my director. After a while I was amazed at how many examples I was storing up! I wasn't 'the brightest bulb on the tree', but I was learning so much. What my director had done was raise my awareness of how much learning I was exposed to every hour of my day.

1.10

Work to live – live to work

Work-life balance has always been a big issue. Go back in history and you find that many people worked long and punishing hours. Look around the world and you'll see the same lack of balance in many people's lives. So what balance should we have?

If you have a problem getting the balance right, then I would point you to the website www.worklifebalance.com. They have three simple statements about this subject:

■ **Work-life balance does not mean an equal balance.** Scheduling an equal number of hours for each of your various work and personal activities is unrealistic. Life should be more fluid than that.

■ **Your best individual work-life balance will vary over time, often on a daily basis.** The right balance for you today will probably be different for you tomorrow. The right balance when you are single will be different if you have a partner or have children.

■ **There is no perfect, one-size fits all, balance you should be striving for.** The best work-life balance is different for each of us because we all have different priorities and different lives.

A wonderful boss I had when I was just starting work told me: "You never get something for nothing. Everything has a price." Over the years his words have stayed with me. Do what you want to do, but be willing to pay the price for it.

The work-life balance website agrees: "Achievement and enjoyment are the front and back of the coin of value in life. You can't have one without the other, no more than you can have a coin with only one side. Trying to live a one-sided life is why so many 'successful' people are not happy, or not nearly as happy as they should be."

Yes, the organization and you have a responsibility to help employees achieve a balance. But we all have an individual responsibility to ourselves to ensure that our personal needs and wants are met.

A work-life balance will constantly change according to different factors in your home and working life.

Leadership responsi-
bilities

Is leadership different from management? My conviction is that it is. A company appoints a leader because it has expectations. This chapter begins by clarifying those expectations and examining how to deliver against them. We then explore the range of behaviours required in a leader – taking command one moment, then demonstrating genuine humility the next, employing the right approach that restores a team to its previous effectiveness.

2.1

Transform the abstract into concrete

Leadership theories are everywhere – the Internet, books, television. But let's ignore the experts' theories for a moment and get back to the basics. Let's look at what your company wants from you. After all, they're the ones paying your salary.

Companies have expectations of their leaders. I believe their expectations are usually that you will deliver the following:

1 Look to the future and anticipate how you think things will look. Can you describe it out loud to someone? What challenges will there be in this future?

2 Decide how your team or department should position itself to meet this future. What will the requirements be? What resources will you need? What won't you need?

3 Turn this abstract future into something concrete. Describe it in outcomes, challenges and tasks. Plan the journey. Set out milestones along the route of the journey.

"We must become the change we want to see"

Mahatma Gandhi, leader of the Indian independence movement

4 Describe this future and journey to your team. Communicate in detail what success will look like and why. Show them the journey and milestones. Get their input.

5 Motivate your team towards this future. Convince hearts and minds that this is where the team must go. They must be emotionally committed – not just intellectually committed.

6 Agree concrete actions. Turn goals into measurable objectives. Turn objectives into personal targets. The team has to share ownership of this journey with you. They have a map. Now's the time to start walking!

7 Make sure you keep people on the right journey. You must ensure that everyone's efforts are in the right direction. You don't walk ahead. You don't walk behind. You walk together.

8 Evaluate the journey as you all walk along it. How well is the journey going? Have we missed anything? Do we need to adjust our plan? Are we sure we're keeping to the right route?

On the way the leader must make sure that the team is prepared to meet this future, building up their confidence and providing them with new skills through training and development.

You must anticipate the future and prepare your team to meet it.

2.2

Lead but don't forget to manage

One question that always comes up is: "What's the difference between managing and leading?" Does it matter? Well, I think it does. I think clarifying the difference helps you see leadership in a clearer way. Some people say they want to be leaders, not managers. I say you have to be both. Let me tell you why.

The problem starts with the words 'manager' and 'leader'. Why are senior people called 'managers' when what you want is leadership? Why do team leaders, who are often junior, have 'leader' in their job title when their focus must be on managing?

one minute wonder So are you a manager or a leader? What tasks do you do which are management tasks? What tasks do you do which are leadership tasks? What is the expectation of your role? Managing or leading? How close do you come to delivering what's expected of your role?

"You manage things; you lead people" Grace Murray Hopper, pioneer computer scientist

You have to forget job titles and concentrate on the words as verbs. Abraham Zaleznik, a respected theorist on the subject of leadership thought that the role of a leader was like "...an artist, scientist, and creative thinker as opposed to a manager". Managers live in – and maintain – the system, the detail of working life. The small stuff. They're responsible for the ship's boilers. They make sure the turbines are working. See to it that the crew's happy and that courses are followed. But the leader decides the course. They look at the map and place their finger on where the ship is going.

Much of the literature on the subject implies that leadership is sexy and management is dull. In your current job it's probably true that both roles are expected of you. The company wants you to decide your team's direction, but also wants you to make sure the team is doing the detail. These contrasting definitions may help to clarify the roles.

- Managers plan detail; leaders set direction.
- Managers focus on getting work completed; leaders focus on leading people.
- Managers create stability; leaders create change.
- Managers have short-term horizons; leaders have long-term horizons.

Think about writer Peter Drucker's famous quote: "Management is doing things right; leadership is doing the right things."

Managers concentrate on detail whilst leaders concentrate on change.

2.3

Lead to bring about 'climate change'

Business environments are constantly changing. Sometimes it can change from hour to hour, and a leader has to develop a weather vane to detect which way the business wind is blowing. As soon as they detect storm clouds ahead, they have to be able to use a leadership style that gets the climate back to sunny and warm.

This use of the word 'climate' for the working environment was proposed by psychologists Litwin and Stringer. They identified six key factors that influence this environment:

■ Its flexibility – that is, how free are employees to innovate?
■ What sense of responsibility do employees have to the organization?
■ What level of standards are people set?
■ How accurate and detailed is performance feedback?
■ How clear are people about the company's mission and values?
■ What level of commitment do the team have to the common purpose?

"The wise adapt themselves to circumstances, as water moulds itself to the pitcher" **Chinese proverb**

Research found that six distinctive leadership styles had a profound effect on this 'climate' and that only the best leaders knew when to use the right style to have the greatest positive impact.

- **Coercive leaders** demand immediate compliance.
- **Authoritative leaders** mobilize people towards a vision.
- **Affiliative leaders** create emotional bonds and harmony.
- **Democratic leaders** build consensus through participation.
- **Pace-setting leaders** expect excellence and self-direction.
- **Coaching leaders** develop people for the future.

Some of these styles you'll recognize in yourself. But are there any styles you never use? When facing situations that demand a particular approach, using the wrong style could prove disastrous. What if the team has had a setback and morale is low? Using a coercive style might create completely the wrong outcome: "Get real, people. If you don't get back to reality, I'll give you something real to worry about!" In fact, the only time I'd use a coercive style is with a problem employee. And even then I'd use it carefully.

In fact, the research established that the authoritative leadership style has the most positive effect on most climates. But three others – affiliative, democratic and coaching – aren't far behind. That said, no style should be used exclusively, and all have at least short-term uses.

The best leaders know which style to employ to create the best team climate.

2.4

Be confident as a strong leader

When you become a leader you get used to assuming command. If your journey looks as if it might be wandering off course, then you swiftly – and effectively – use your leadership skills to get things back on track. These are the qualities and attitudes that will help you confidently take control of the situation.

■ **You just love leading.** You feel 'at home' in these tough situations. You know it's going to play to your leadership strengths.

■ **You're ready to be unpopular** (if that's what it takes). When the sea gets choppy, only the strongest can keep that tiller steady.

■ **You confront difficulties.** You walk out to meet the problem head-on. You have enough self-belief to know you're going to overcome it.

"To command is to serve, nothing more and nothing less"

André Malraux, French writer and politician

one minute wonder When was the last time you saw someone who had to reassert control over a situation? Perhaps it was your boss, or a manager of another team? How well did they do it? Did they rise to meet the situation or back away? Did they take responsibility or hide from it? Did they keep cool or bite anyone's head off who questioned them? There's a lot to be learned from how others have dealt with tough situations.

■ **You love challenges.** Rather than look to avoid tough situations, you know that they bring out some great qualities that you have. You see the challenge as a chance to dust off those skills.

■ **You're the person that everyone turns to.** When things gets tough, your team wants you on their side. They know you have the personal strength to make it through a tough time.

■ **You create open and honest discussion.** You don't skirt around the issue. If it's bad news then you want it straight. You know that you have to have an accurate idea of what you're dealing with.

■ **You are cool under pressure.** When the heat is on, you stay calm. When someone loses self-control, you respond intelligently and coolly.

■ **You stay focused on the right things.** A crisis often makes weaker leaders question their goals. A great leader maintains self-belief in themselves and the goals that they're focusing on.

Be prepared to reassume command when difficult situations develop.

2.5

Have enough humility to avoid humiliation

A leader be humble? Have you read that right? Leaders are dynamic, strong-minded, focused… and occasionally wrong. Having humility is not thinking less of ourselves. It's more about thinking of ourselves less. It's about stimulating conversations that allow people to confront the truth rather than skirting diplomatically around it.

The trouble with humility is that if you think you already have it – you probably don't. A leader who has this gift of humility realizes that they are surrounded by a team. The team doesn't exist to worship the leader. The team exists as 'peers-in-thinking'. People the leader works with to make goals materialize.

Can I teach you humility? No. But I can tell you how people with humility behave.

■ **They are genuinely open to the views of others.** They investigate opinions that counter their own. What's more, they willingly give ground when persuaded.

"It is always the secure who are humble"

G. K. Chesterton, English writer and journalist

■ **When they know they're not right, they concede.** Some leaders who lack humility hate to be seen to be wrong. They see winning as preferable to establishing the truth.

■ **They are open about their faults to others.** They might as well own up, their team probably spotted them long ago!

■ **They're ready to 'roll up their sleeves' with the rest.** If the whole team's under pressure, then they'll play their part to get the task done.

■ **They don't let their opinion take precedence over others' opinions.** They wait in line. They also know that others' thoughts may well alter their opinion anyway.

■ **They're gracious when others are praised over them.** They're secure enough to know that every skill they have is performed better by someone else out there. They're comfortable with that.

■ **They don't equate possessions with worth.** Others will have a better car, nicer house, earn more. These aren't indicators of personal worth. They prefer to judge people by who they are – not what they own.

But don't think that humility is another word for 'being a wimp'. A tenacious, highly respected, demanding leader can still possess humility. It ensures that they don't live in a bunker pretending that the war above them is going to plan. Humility brings reality right into their office. It stops them making decisions that would bring a humiliating reality crashing around their ears.

Humility is about thinking about ourselves less.

2.6

Open up to people

I work a lot with front-line staff. When I ask them to
list the qualities of their favourite leader, one word is
always in the top three. That word is 'approachable'.
Why do some leaders see this as something not to be
encouraged? Good leaders know that it opens up one
of the best information channels of all.

Some leaders think of the role as being one of mystery. The
general standing alone at the top of the hill. Lost in profound thoughts.
Tortured by the heavy responsibility resting on their shoulders.

Be a lonely tortured leader if you want. But don't expect that to
make you a good leader. Good leaders know decisions are helped by
access to the best information. And the information is out there. You
have to make sure it wants to come up and make itself known to you.
Here are seven proven ways to make sure you're approachable to people.

1 **Have time for people.** If you're in a rush ask if you can catch
up later. Then make sure that you do!

2 **Approach people.** Get them used to being in your company.
Stimulate conversation so that they feel at ease with you.

"I try to keep an open mind, but not so open that my brains fall out" Richard Feynman, American scientist and raconteur

3 **Be aware of your body language.** Don't send the wrong signals. Putting on your coat as you ask, "Tell me all about it" is not a good approach.

4 **Smile.** One of the most welcoming ways one human shows another how glad they are to see them. Don't believe me? Try smiling when you're talking to someone you can't stand.

5 **Don't just talk about work.** Be sociable. Show them that you have a home life too!

6 **Listen, listen, listen!** Concentrate on the message. Don't think "Oh, not them again…" Even deeply irritating people often have some great insights.

7 **Give out genuine compliments.** It's not flattery. That's when you give false compliments. But being complimentary shows respect and admiration.

All managers who have an open-door policy will close their door at times. Make it a rare event, but do use it when you need to be private. Being approachable and always being available are two different things.

Being approachable ensures that all feedback channels remain open to you.

Leadership strategy

Ready for the big idea? If you truly see yourself as a leader then you'll have to develop and implement a strategy. To do this, you need to think in terms of the 'big picture'. Pull yourself away from the day-to-day so you can look at the 'year-to-year'. You then need to wrap up your strategy in a message that people connect with and work to get it clear of the ground. And once the strategy is airborne you have to keep it there, making sure that the team delivers it.

3.1

Think of forests – not trees

Putting together a strategy places some real demands on a leader's ability to think in the widest sense. Some are great at the immediate issues – the 'here and now' stuff. But they struggle to think about how things interconnect. Organizations are complicated. And the ability of a leader to appreciate and respond to this complexity is essential.

Peter Senge, the American who developed the dynamic concept of a "learning organization", argued that much of management and

case study Let me take you out of the office to show how action meant to solve something can actually make it much worse. The traditional approach to dealing with crop damage is to use insecticides. A crop spray kills the insect damaging the crop, the crop yields will be greater and everyone's happy. Except it doesn't happen like that. In the short term, the effects are better. But soon enough the crop damage gets

leadership theory is simplistic. It encourages us to concentrate only on 'parts'. His ideal model for an organization is one where the leaders are able to see the system in its entirety and are aware that an adjustment in one part of the system may have a significant effect on something else.

Some people just can't do this. They focus their energies on one small area of the strategy, without seeing how it interacts with other areas. As the saying goes, "They can't see the wood for the trees."

Senge pointed out that: "We learn best from our experience, but we never directly experience the consequences of many of our most important decisions." Haven't you known people who had an eye-catching short-term solution to something, which eventually proved costly? (See the case study below.)

His argument is that leaders must see – and consider – the whole strategy. Concentrate on the interfaces and boundaries of components. Be sensitive to their connections and influence on each other.

You have to be able to view the strategy in its entirety and see how all parts of it interconnect.

worse – worse than the damage levels before the insecticide was used. So what happened? It seems that the insect also controlled the population of yet another insect. The population of this insect – with no predator to keep it in check – explodes and suddenly you have a bigger problem than before! Studies show that a majority of the insects that cause the most crop damage became problems because of this cycle.

3.2

Avoid a short-sighted vision

It's a tale of two strategies. The strategy your company has set its sights on delivering. And the strategy you want your team to deliver. Both strategies have to be complementary. So when you start thinking about your strategy, make sure you've done your organizational homework first.

Strategy has been defined as "the direction and scope of an organization over the long-term". How do you develop your strategy? You need to consider three important questions.

1 **Where are you now?** Think carefully about how your area of the operation sits at the moment.

2 **Where are the opportunities for you to grow?** If you've good business acumen then you'll have already made mental notes of some possible answers.

3 **What is the strategy of the organization?** What are its big themes? How can your strategy meet its long-term objective?

"The very essence of leadership is that you have to have vision. You can't blow an uncertain trumpet"

Theodore Hesburgh, American activist Catholic priest

Answers to these questions will help you form your own operational strategy. Once you have the strategy you'll need to wrap it up in something that people can remember: your strategic vision. This is a statement of your long-term intent. It's going to have to include:

- A well-defined common direction.
- The destination that lies over the horizon.
- The constraints you'll be working under.
- The critical issues that will be addressed.
- The programmes that will be employed to achieve the strategy.

But I said that there were two strategies. One is the overall organizational strategy. You should have this committed to memory! Then there's your strategy. How your area is going to contribute towards the organizational strategy. And this fit is crucial. One has to be in harmony with the other. For example, if the organizational strategy is chasing volume and yours is concentrating on creating higher-value business then there are going to be problems. Two conflicting strategies will be pulling in different directions.

And strategies are not fixed. They are constantly renewed as the environment the organization operates in continues to change.

Your strategy must show how it will contribute to the company's long-term organizational strategy.

3.3

Strategy: get it into their heads

There's research that suggests that less than 5% of people in any organization know what its strategy is. If true, that's a worrying statistic. A strategy that sits only in the heads of the people who developed it is a dream. Successfully communicating the strategy is the act of breathing life into your strategic ambition.

So let's look at ways that really get your strategy into the heads of your people.

■ **Create a strategy presentation and deliver it.** Use techniques that help the strategy 'come alive' for people. Think of approaches that people will enjoy and engage with.

■ **Keep it concentrated on key top-line themes.** There's probably going to be a lot of complexity behind the strategy. Think about the big stuff that lets people know the broad strategic intentions.

■ **Communicate how the strategy will affect them.** Sell the positive impact, the benefits they'll see.

■ **Paint pictures for people.** Human beings love pictures! Describe the promised land. Paint the future. Help people see what you're aiming for.

■ **Express your objectives in measurable terms.** Objectives that lack measures will appear vague. You want people to see the 'stretch' you're asking of them.

■ **Anticipate objections.** Use rhetorical questions to overcome objections. "Now I know you're thinking, 'Surely now's not the time to do this.' But let me show you why now's the perfect time…"

■ **Have an easy-to-read summary of the strategy as a handout.** People need to be able to read it quickly, so make sure the document is concise. Even a one-sheet summary might be enough.

■ **Think carefully about what they need to know.** You don't want to put anything confidential in there but you also have to make sure it's not so censored that it tells people nothing.

People 'buy in' to a strategy when they are intellectually and emotionally convinced. Doing the above will help make sure that you achieve this. Now ownership of the strategy will sit with everyone.

Present the key elements of your strategy with a one-page overview that will make it available to everyone.

3.4

Turn your strategy into action

You have your strategy and have communicated it to the team. But research shows that the success for implementing a new strategy is depressingly low. Figures range between 10 – 30%. So what can the leader do to make sure that this abstract strategy translates into real actions and results?

We spoke in Chapter 2 about the difference between leadership and management. The 'doing the right things' against 'doing things right'. Now we have to concentrate on the latter. We need to ensure we carefully manage the implementation of the strategy. This involves:

■ **Putting the right resources in place.** This means people, money, technology and whatever resource is going make the strategy happen.
■ **Having a detailed action plan.** There will be a lot of tasks and processes which will need assigning to those who are going to make this happen. Outcomes must be specific and clear.
■ **Developing a clear communication structure.** Continuing to get the strategic message 'out there' demands clear lines of communication. You'll also need this for the feedback loop back to the leader.

"It is not enough to stare up the steps – we must step up the stairs" **Vance Havner, American revivalist preacher**

■ **Constructing an accurate monitoring process.** You have to make sure that the strategy is happening. How can you build in early-warning alarms? What if the strategy starts to go 'off track'?

We started out saying that implementation is tough. Most strategies hit obstacles and you have to be ready to deal with them as they happen. You really have three choices.

1 **You alter the delivery date.** You're still maintaining the right course, you're just going to have to accept that it's a longer journey than you realized.

2 **You change tactics.** Perhaps your initial choice of tactics was not as sound as you thought? Better to revisit those tactics and rethink them.

3 **You change the strategy.** Hands up. It was the wrong strategy in the first place. There's no shame in this. The world changes so quickly that right strategies very quickly look like seriously wrong strategies.

Strategies are easier to create than they are to implement. You have to move from future thinking to thinking about the 'now'.

All strategies hit obstacles, so be ready to act quickly when they do.

3.5

Be a business expert

Some people see business acumen as something you gain from reading books. You need to be reading more than books. You need to be reading the business landscape. Analysing where the opportunities are and taking advantage of the opportunities that arise. Here's a guide to where those who lack business acumen go wrong.

■ **They don't understand the market forces and other factors that drive their business.** What are the 'drivers' in your business? Write them down. They'll help you focus on important activities.

■ **They don't read.** Thinking is moving all the time. Reading helps you know what's new in your working life.

one minute wonder When was the last time you attended a learning event related to your own work? When was the last time you read an article that expanded your business thinking? How much encouragement do you give your team to develop their business acumen? What are the first signs that tell you when it's lacking in someone?

"Man's mind, once stretched by a new idea, never regains its original dimensions"

Oliver Wendell Holmes, American author and physician

■ **They don't think outside their own office.** Every job exists in a bigger context. It's vital to know how what you do affects others.

■ **They don't understand the broader strategy.** They can't make the link between their world and how it contributes to the organization's purpose.

■ **They don't have an appetite for learning.** It's vital to want to understand. To be curious. To find things out. They're essential components of a person's growth.

■ **They have no interest in competitors.** There is always something you can learn from those who operate in your marketplace. Even if it's why they are still lagging behind you!

Business acumen helps you concentrate on connecting what you do with opportunities that arise. As business thinker Ram Charan points out, business acumen is "…an insightful assessment of the external business landscape with the keen awareness of how money can be made – and then executing the strategy to deliver the desired results".

Having business acumen raises the respect others have for you. It means that your suggestions are based on a wide and thorough experience of the business environment you operate in.

Leaders with business acumen know their territory and how to thrive in it.

Leadership
and execution

Leadership is about 'unknowns'. You will have to make some tough decisions in situations that are hard to predict and understand. Few strategies go exactly to plan and that's where the learning and growing happens – dealing with setbacks you encounter along the way. Then we'll look at how your team executes its tasks and ways of monitoring their performance. Then there are also the people outside the team you're going to have to collaborate with.

4.1

Get tough with tough decisions

Television often shows the leader coolly striding through the office. Some executive rushes up with a problem and the leader quickly sends them on their way. Another great decision made. But real life is so different. Decision-making for a leader is tough because they deal with greater unknowns. And the consequences are all the greater too.

The book *Culture and Leadership across the World* (see Further reading) conducted extensive research into decision-making. It showed that the most difficult decisions are related to personal matters (46%). Second were economic and financing decisions (18%). Last came legal

one minute wonder How does your boss deal with tough decisions? Which of this Secret's recommendations do they follow? What strategy do they use to make a tough call? Can you learn from them? Are there errors they make in their decision-making that are useful lessons in what not to do?

> "Cowardice asks the question: Is it safe? Consensus asks the question: Is it popular? Conscience asks: Is it right?" **Martin Luther King, Jr, American civil rights leader**

ambiguities (16%) and organizational conflicts (6%). The difficult decisions were those associated with the future of people. Things like disciplinary decisions or making staff redundant. So, when you have a tough decision to make, consider the following.

■ **Decide if it's really your decision.** Has someone 'passed the buck' to avoid the decision themselves? Deal only with your own decisions.

■ **Do your research.** The worst decisions are often made because all of the pieces of the problem were not considered. If you're missing key information, what chance will you have?

■ **Identify the choices before you.** All decision making is about choice. Look at the alternatives and satisfy yourself that these are the only options.

■ **Look for assistance from other skilled decision makers.** This isn't some sort of climb-down. You have experience you can call on out there, so be strong and consult.

■ **Take your time.** OK, this isn't always possible. But often there is time and time is what's needed most with tough decisions.

■ **Consider the timing of your decision.** When's the best time to implement? There are good – and bad – times to execute your decision.

■ **Think about your beliefs and values.** They're often a reliable compass that can guide your decision-making.

Avoid making hasty, ill-informed decisions. The most difficult ones are those that affect people's lives.

4.2

Deliver or die

Getting people to agree to tasks is relatively easy. But you need to get them to deliver those tasks on time and to a standard you're happy with. First they need to be working on the right things in the right way. Next they must hit the deadlines you've agreed with them.

After all, your reputation stands or falls on your team's ability to deliver. So what can you do to make sure everyone executes tasks competently and on time?

1 **Recruit people with a history of achievement.** When interviewing, make sure you press for examples of real achievement in their previous roles. Ask questions that begin with "Tell me about a time when..."

2 **Ask task owners to share their plan with you.** Agree an outcome and leave the path to be taken to be decided by the task owner. But make sure they share that plan beforehand.

3 **Make sure commitments are followed through.** Check that people deliver within the timescale they promised.

4 **Make sure commitments are achieved ethically.** When someone delivers on a commitment that's great. But if, in doing so, they've left a trail of unhappy people in their wake, then you've got trouble.

5 **Encourage people to be decisive.** You're not always around, so you need people to make decisions that keep things moving. Train them to do so. It's a skill that deepens with practice.

6 **Deal firmly with time wasting.** Some people fail to deliver their task because they manage their workload so poorly. Coach people with workload management problems.

7 **Treat people as individuals.** High performers with a history of task achievement will receive more trust then the new kid on the block. Respect – and respond to – the competency levels of the individual.

A recent global productivity report found that employees were spending more than a third of their time on unproductive activities. That's the equivalent of 1.7 days a week on stuff that doesn't deliver!

Make sure your team delivers.

4.3

Mind your way through 'roadblocks'

However much we try it's impossible to forecast everything. As sure as night follows day, we know 'roadblocks' are going to appear. This is all a normal part of leadership. However, our attitude to these roadblocks influences the success we have getting over, around or through them.

In my own experience, roadblocks have a lot to do with the way people look at them. Some see them as normal events that occur when you're trying to change things. Others see them as demotivating 'dead ends' that leave them holding their heads in their hands.

So when you get a roadblock, first decide exactly what the roadblock is. I have based the following descriptions on original work by Frank Navran.

1   **The brick wall.** These are real and solid. It's no use wishing them away, they can't be moved. Examples are your budget being slashed or key people assigned to another project. They're beyond your control and you have to think smart about how you deal with them.

"Some are destined to succeed, some are determined to succeed"

H. H. Swami Tejomayananda, Indian spiritual leader

2 **The partition.** Like a real partition, if you push it from the bottom then it will move slightly. But push it from the top and you can topple it over. As you're 'higher up' in the organization you may well be the person to do that for them. Smarter leaders consider whether there's a way around it rather than deal with it 'head on'.

3 **The paper wall.** Think of the entertainer who bursts through a paper circle and gets the crowd cheering. A paper wall looks solid to the employee, but all it takes is the courage to show that it's no roadblock at all. Examples are sentences like: "No one's ever done it that way." "You won't get the 'buy in' from the senior team." They exist only in the mind of the person looking at the roadblock.

4 **The mindset.** When someone tells you they can't overcome the roadblock, they're right. Their 'self-talk' is preventing them. An internal dialogue presenting them with reason after reason why something's not going to happen. You must change this mindset to one that seeks to overcome the roadblock – not shrink from it.

The size and solidity of a roadblock often depend on the mindset of the person viewing it.

4.4

Collaborate and make everyone happy

Organizations have changed so much. Some still keep their hierarchy. But others have increasingly moved to different, more complex, structures. This means that their leaders have to develop new skills to achieve their goals. One of the most vital of these skills is the ability to collaborate strategically with others across the organization.

Collaboration is where two or more leaders work together towards a common goal. It demands that both break away from a departmental focus to one that is shared. But both don't just share the goal, they also share the risk.

case study During a recent collaboration workshop a marketing director came up and said, "I work with a sales director and there's no collaboration at all. We spend our time just scoring points off each other." I asked how long this had been going on. "About six months." Had he ever tried to collaborate? "Surely

And this is where collaboration can go wrong. If the project fails, collaboration can turn into a 'blame game'. So let's look at how you can preserve the spirit of true collaboration.

■ **Make every conversation a 'win-win'.** When you collaborate you have to harness both areas of expertise to create real benefits for all.

■ **Get to know the other leader's perspective.** Understand how they view the common goal. Learn about their concerns and find out what their capabilities are.

■ **Make sure that you are all clear about the common goal.** This is vital. Keep it as your common focus point.

■ **Be flexible.** There's often a lot of 'blurring' over who is responsible for what. Get comfortable with this and encourage a 'give and take' mentality.

■ **Both sides have to be equally committed.** Make sure both teams share an equal and mutual feeling of respect for each other.

■ **Have clear communication processes.** No time for 'knowledge is power'! You have to share knowledge openly. Decision-making and other processes should be agreed ahead of the collaboration.

Change your focus from a departmental one to that of working together to achieve a shared organizational goal.

that's down to her? I'm the new director. Not her." I asked if collaboration could only be initiated by the more experienced director. And how much his marketing strategy's success depended on her sales team? We met the next day. He'd called her the night before. "We needed to start again," he said.

4.5

Fight battles worth winning

A large army can be fighting on several fronts. The challenge for the leader is to know where to direct their forces. You've probably felt the same dilemma. You can't divide yourself up and confront every obstacle in your path. So you must choose carefully which battles you intend to fight.

The inexperienced leader fights every battle. This drains energy, demoralizing both them and their team. As Sun Tzu, the Ancient Chinese author of *The Art of War*, advises, "…choose your battles wisely" and "do not fight battles you cannot win". Here are some questions to help prioritize your 'must-win battles'.

■ **Will the battle benefit your goals?** Remember General Rommel's advice: "Don't fight a battle if you don't gain anything by winning." No real benefits? Then why get involved?
■ **If you can't do anything about the outcome, is it better to forget it?** You might get satisfaction 'letting off steam', but is it really worth it?

"Win as if you were used to it, lose as if you enjoyed it for a change" Ralph Waldo Emerson, American philosopher

■ **Will the battle actually solve something?** Are you just trying to correct a wrong, or will the outcome be worthwhile?

■ **Has the battle anything to do with you?** Yes, the colleague has your support. But will getting involved deflect you from your goals? Let people fight their own fights.

■ **Have you assessed what the battle is really about?** Are you mad because your boss withdrew that promised resource, or is it really that they don't give your projects the same priority as others?

■ **How important will you think this battle will be in the future?** In six months time, if you struggled to recall the issue, what will that tell you about its importance?

■ **Is it better to just walk away?** Some people have to have the last word. You're the better leader for letting it go and concentrating your energies on other priorities.

Fighting every battle may earn you a reputation as a confrontational person. It also can create enemies of people you're going to need further down the road. So decide the two or three vital battles you need to win.

Leadership is about taking the long view. There are battles you fight today because you know they're vital to what you're trying to achieve. But there are also battles you leave for later.

Reserve your battles for the issues that are vital to your goals.

4.6

Recruit and encourage 'response-ability'

When things go wrong in your team what happens? Do people look for someone to blame? Blaming others is a waste of everyone's time. It also means you lack 'response-ability'. The ability to take ownership and select the right response in a situation.

Ask your employees if they have free will. Most will say 'yes'. They believe they have control of the choices life puts before them and take responsibility for what they do and most of what happens to them.

Others may tell you that they have no control (see the case study below). But not good people. In a tricky situation good people immediately think about solutions. They own the issue and feel responsible for solving it. They have response–ability.

---

case study Some employees accept no responsiblity for what they do and are always ready to blame external forces. "Niamh, are those figures ready yet?" "You know I'm trying to get this customer's proposal ready. I haven't even had a chance to look at the

---

"When the ball is coming over the net, you can be sure I want the ball" **Billie Jean King, tennis champion**

In his book *The Luck Factor*, Richard Wiseman defined four attributes of people who take responsibility – not only for their work – but also for their lives.

■ **They frequently find chance opportunities.** They're open and receptive to possibilities and spot opportunities others miss.

■ **They listen to their hunches.** They follow hunches and gut feelings. And these pay off time and again.

■ **They persevere in the face of failure.** They believe everything will work out eventually for them. What's more, they're often right!

■ **They turn bad luck into good fortune.** Every disaster is somehow turned to their advantage. They learn from what they do wrong.

These are the people you want in your team. When you recruit, make sure that you look for this talent. Ask for examples of overcoming setbacks or what various disappointments have taught them.

Recruit people with the ability to choose the right response from a range of possibilities.

figures." Notice the self-justifying "...haven't even had a chance to look at the figures". The matter was completely out of her hands. Some people always play this card. They believe they have no choice and can't be held responsible when things go wrong.

4.7

Respond to underperfomance

When a leader discovers someone underperforming, it's a critical moment. You often experience a dangerous mixture of stress and rising dissatisfaction. Controlling these difficult emotions and managing your response is crucial. You don't want to underperform when challenged by underperformance.

So let's be careful before we wade in with a big stick. Everyone underperforms at one time or another. First establish whether this is going to be a 'one off' instance or if it's the beginning of a permanent level of performance.

If it's a 'one off' then you can probably have a quiet word and move on. But if it's part of pattern of underperformance then you're going to need to take swift action. But let me give you some advice. Whatever you do, pay close attention to your emotional state.

As soon as you feel under emotional pressure of this kind there's a part of your brain that wants to take over. It's called the amygdala and it's just itching to pull a trigger. This trigger floods the body with adrenalin. And adrenalin gets you heated! So you have to control it – and therefore control yourself.

"He who angers you conquers you"

Elizabeth Kenny, Australian pioneering physical therapist

How do you do it? It's easier then you think. For example, I ask Alfonso for the promised management report but he starts to ask for another week to complete it. I shout: "Another week! Are you kidding? You've messing up big time, Alfonso!" Not good. Now they're under-performing and demotivated. You have twice the problem you had before you answered. I didn't respond to Alfonso, I reacted.

Reactions place my behaviour into other people's hands. I prefer to take responsibility for my behaviour. So, even when I feel anger, I remain calm and respond with a question. "Alfonso, I know you're under pressure with this, but another week's too long. When's the earliest time you can have a draft to me?"

Yes, you want to scream. But you also need that report quickly. If I upset Alfonso so much he doesn't show up next day then I've an even bigger problem getting my report. In some countries, failing to deal calmly with just this sort of underperformance issue can land you in deep trouble.

When upset by underperformance, respond with a question. Always avoid emotionally driven reactions.

4.8

Negate the negative conflict

You must avoid conflict. Right? Wrong. Conflict can be healthy. But a leader must recognize – and quickly deal with – any destructive conflict. This type of conflict has a nasty habit of disrupting the team's progress towards their goals. Here are seven important ways to help you avoid any destructive conflict.

1 **Have regular one-to ones with the people you lead.** It's a great way to 'test the water' about how people are feeling. Often employees may be more open than in a team session.

2 **Be clear about roles and responsibilities.** Conflict often arises because the leader hasn't set these out carefully. People need their roles and responsibilities clarified, especially in looser hierarchies or matrix environments.

3 **Anticipate and deal with any underlying tensions.** Don't wait for bombs to be dropped. Destroy the aircraft before they reach your territory. Think ahead and deal with the issues you know will arise.

4 **Be consultative in day-to-day decision making.** Some decisions belong to you. But there are many others you can consult on. It will also help staff see – and experience – the consequences of those decisions.

5 **Manage the expectations of the team.** Don't wait for things to happen, be up-front about possible problems that may arise from decisions so that people can prepare.

6 **Watch for signs of stress in employees.** You know how your people look when they're happy. So recognize the signals when they're stressed. Don't wait – deal with it immediately.

7 **Manage disruptive employees firmly.** We all have them. The cynical employee that can damage team spirit. Make sure they're 'on message' about your goals and direction.

But you mustn't always avoid conflict. There's a lot of good conflict you need to encourage. A team meeting can be all the healthier when important issues are debated with passion. You don't want to kill this. It's a chance to understand the real issues in the workplace.

Anticipate harmful conflict, but encourage passionate debate.

Leadership
and change

You'll see a link here with some of the techniques we discussed in Chapter 3. But this chapter concentrates on the delivery of smaller changes resulting from the organization's change in strategy. People don't hate change as such. But they do hate change they don't understand or don't agree with. So selling the change is essential. You have to make them want to go with you, deal with their anxieties and respect the emotions that change stirs up.

5.1

Develop a vision of change everyone sees

Most visions are handed down to staff. Many of the standard texts on managing change talk about 'communicating your vision'. But isn't it better to make it 'our vision'? Not only will it secure wider commitment to making it come true. You'll also have created a team of believers ready to go out and sell it.

Whether you're leading a group of managers or just your own team through change, the goal is the same. To develop a destination that you all need to reach. A place where things will be very different to what they are now. This destination – or vision – should be as Gary Yukl, author of *Leadership in Organizations*, defined it: "An image of what can be achieved, why it is worthwhile, and how it can be done." Here are some pointers to help create that vision.

■ **It must be concise.** Remembered the elevator sell? You have a couple of floors to sell your idea to the person in the elevator with you. That's how short the vision has to be.

one minute wonder What is the next major change you want to introduce? Who can you involve in developing the vision? How would you structure the vision meeting? What are the obstacles you might encounter? How comfortable would you feel sharing this responsibility?

■ **It must describe an attractive destination.** A trip to a holiday destination not to the dentist's. What does your vision sound like?

■ **It must have conviction.** It's a better place to be than where we are now. That's why I am driven by the motivation to get there.

■ **It must be realistic.** It's not a dream that could never happen. It's rooted in a reality that I know can happen.

■ **It must be adaptable.** Things change. And if they do, there's enough adaptability in the vision that it can accommodate or adapt to that change.

■ **It must be easy to understand.** It doesn't use highly technical or inaccessible language. It communicates directly with everyone.

So what about an example? "Within two years we will have increased our revenues from the public sector by 30% and be seen as the principal supplier of office equipment to this sector. This will be achieved from a focused campaign of sales penetration and a commitment to creating long lasting and mutually profitable relationships with buyers in the industry."

Your vision must set out the destination you want to reach and why it's worth reaching.

5.2

Convince people why they must change

We've looked at strategic planning in Chapter 3. It's the big, long-term direction that says where the organization – and your part of it – is heading over the coming months or years. But now we need to turn to more immediate matters. Operational changes that you want to put into place that may need to be implemented in just months, or weeks.

The change might be the introduction of a new piece of software. Developing a totally different way of dealing with customers. Restructuring the team to respond to new business developments. Whatever it is, it has to be communicated to an audience for the first time.

case study In my early career I worked at a Ford Car dealership. Dave, the workshop manager asked his technicians to a meeting. He said people weren't having their cars repaired at the dealership because smaller rivals did it cheaper. He prepared a PowerPoint presentation contrasting falling revenues with rising

"The longest journey of any person is the journey inward"

Dag Hammerskjvld, Swedish author

But people are going to ask questions like, "What's wrong with the way we do it now?" and "Why change?" Therefore you have three important things to achieve when you kick off any change process.

1 **Why the change is needed.** You must prove why the current state is not good enough any more. If you don't convince them of this then implementation will be so much tougher.

2 **Where it is you are heading for.** Not only what it will look like, but the benefits it will bring for everyone. Remember, they're going to ask themselves, "What's in it for me?"

3 **The journey that will need to be undertaken.** A logical process that moves the group towards the new state.

What is crucial is for the leader to create tension between stages one and three. If employees are not convinced of the need for change, then they're not going to move.

You have to convince people why they need to stop their current practices.

rents, overheads and salaries. If they didn't reorganize and perform better, they were 'dead in the water'. After a shocked silence, Dave asked for their commitment. Not only did they rebuild the business, it outperformed other Ford dealerships in their region both on volume and service quality for the next two years.

5.3

Be sensitive to the change process

People deal with change in very different ways. There are many who are open to change and see it as a normal part of working life. There are others who dread it. They experience a sinking feeling the moment anything new is announced and dearly hope that it may never happen.

Being aware of the stages employees can experience during change is important to the leader. It helps them adapt their behaviour better to support and focus their employees. Here are the four stages for you to look for.

1 **Denial.** Although the employees know change is going to happen, they may try to act as if it's not. By not acknowledging the change's existence, they can cling instead to the present.

2 **Resistance.** Eventually denial is replaced by resistance. They will have real anxieties about their status, security or ability to influence. Expect a wide spectrum of behaviour at this point including negativity.

"All is flux; nothing stays still" Heraclitus, Ancient Greek philosopher

3 **Exploration.** The point where the employee accepts that the change will happen. They start to consider their place in the 'new order'. They don't necessarily welcome the change but openly acknowledge its existence.

4 **Commitment.** They can work effectively in the new situation. They will feel their motivation return as they master the new tasks and processes. Eventually they look outward again – rather than fix on their own anxieties.

This process of change is often shown as a U-shaped curve. At first, when people are informed of the change, morale and motivation go down alarmingly. At the bottom of the 'U' they feel stressed and unproductive. Once they begin to accept the change then it shows in the upward curve. They recover a sense of direction and self-esteem.

But not everyone moves in this logical way through the change curve. Some may become stuck at a certain point. Unable to find the impetus to move on to the next stage. As their leader, you must be sensitive to this. You're also going to have to expect a fall-off in performance as people's motivation decreases. Again this is normal and skilled handling will soon return employees to previous performance levels.

Denial and resistance are normal stages employees go through when struggling with change.

5.4

Maintain momentum

The change process is underway. You've set out the destination. The team has worked with you on putting a plan in place. Now you have to maintain the impetus. Keep motivation high. Make sure other projects and commitments don't deflect people from what you're trying to achieve.

There are three principal areas that you have to work at:

1 **Capability.** Have the team got the right skills to function in the new situation? Are they supported by the right processes? What can I do now to prepare them for the challenges ahead?

2 **Motivation.** Is there the same desire to achieve the change that was present at the outset? Are there things we could implement to maintain that desire? Is there anything that might be demotivating people?

3 **Focus.** Is everyone clear about the specific expectations we've assigned? Are they certain of their responsibilities and what they have to deliver? Is anything deflecting them or causing them to lose focus?

"Let me tell you the secret that has led me to my goal: my strength lies solely in my tenacity"

Louis Pasteur, French chemist

Reassurance that these three factors are present will let you know that the change process is on course. But what else can you do to maintain this momentum?

One tip is to look for 'quick wins' that let people know the process is working. Not only will it fire up the evangelical 'flag-carriers' that you may have, it will send positive messages of success to critics of the initiative. When you develop your initial plans, it's often shrewd to build in these short-term goals. Every 'hit' fills up your employees' tanks with more motivational fuel.

Finally, look for every opportunity to show the team how the change is becoming 'part of the way we do things around here'. Talk about successes. Keep people updated with the benefits the change is creating. Trace any success back to the original goals that were set.

And don't forget to recognize the efforts of those who move the process on. This will encourage them to do the same again and again. When new people come on board, fire them up with the same zeal. They'll pick up the message quickly and make a real contribution to maintaining the impetus of the change.

Highlight any interim successes to keep motivation high and maintain the momentum of change.

5.5

Invite resistance

In an earlier chapter we spoke about roadblocks to a strategy. What if the roadblock is your own people? What if their resistance is so deep-seated that you have a fight on your hands – with your own staff! Well, first you have to identify the causes of their resistance. Here are seven areas of concern where you'll frequently encounter opposition to change.

1 **Employees fear the unknown.** Let's be honest, it's scary to leave everything you know for something you don't yet see. It may exist in the leader's head, but it's not yet lodged in the team's.

2 **You're asking them to be disloyal.** If you're new then you'll know your employees will feel part of a tradition. One you haven't yet understood. Are you asking them to betray the history they've shared?

3 **People don't feel they have the ability to change.** They're not going to tell you this but there will be some who feel they don't have the competence required to survive in the new situation.

4 **People have change fatigue.** Yes, it's all very well to say "change is the only constant" but people can get worn down by it. Yet another change is just change overload.

5 **You've got a secret agenda.** When the change happens, it's going to mean someone losing their job. Or work's going to be doubled. There's something 'nasty in the woodshed' – and you're just not telling them.

6 **They're going to lose status.** In the present set-up they have respect that they've earned over years. Now you're repainting the landscape and they might be reduced to insignificant figures in the background.

7 **They're not convinced by a need to change.** They've heard what you say and they prefer things as they are. What you've envisioned is not a good place to be. They like things this way!

People who fear the unknown or doubt their abilities have a survival anxiety. Whatever the reason for their anxiety, you need to bring it to the surface, acknowledge it openly, reassure them and then move on.

Bring resistance to change out into the open, reassure people that it is only natural and then move on.

5.6

Feedback: watch the ball

You'll always want to know what stage your change process has reached. What shape it's in. How you view the progress of your change initiative will depend on your personal perception of facts, events and results. But perception's a dangerous thing. How can you make sure what you're seeing is really what is happening?

Feedback often supplies the high-quality information you need. But you have to be mature enough to open yourself up to accurate, constructive feedback. Not all leaders have this level of maturity.

Why? Because, for many, when they open themselves up they feel vulnerable. Certain primitive instincts drive them to defend or justify their behaviour. After all, does anyone like to hear criticism about something they've invested so much time in?

We ask for accurate feedback because we're trying to gain a realistic idea of how our change initiative is progressing. If we're able to establish emerging problems early then we can put things right.

"The eye sees only what the mind is prepared to comprehend"

Henri Bergson, French philosopher

What is it that makes a great tennis or squash player? Is it how they hit the ball? No, it is how they pick up the flight of the ball early and move to the best position to hit it. The 'winning shot' begins with the early visual contact they made with the ball.

And this is what accurate feedback is about. It's about getting the important information you need as far ahead as possible. Not when the ball has connected with your racquet. When this happens you're forced to react to events. Pick up the flight of the ball early and then you have choices. So when receiving feedback:

■ Listen carefully and don't react or get defensive.
■ If you hear something you disagree with ask for more information – don't just justify or defend.
■ Control any anger you might feel. Otherwise you'll just close the feedback loop off.
■ Don't think ahead about how to deal with the situation during the feedback. You might miss something crucial.
■ Be detached. Treat the information in an unemotional way.
■ Explore any underlying reasons why the feedback took the form it did.

Accurate feedback allows you to identify emerging problems early and react quicker.

5.7

Accept ambiguity

It's easy to make decisions when you've all the information you need. A little experience, a lot of thought and analysis, and you'll soon arrive at the right choice. But leaders often face new situations with little information and no obvious choices. And as you get higher in the organization, this ambiguity increases.

So who struggles most with ambiguity? In my experience it's the perfectionists. Because perfectionists only think in black and white, they struggle with the greys of real life.

But surely if there was no ambiguity then there would be no learning? Ambiguity stimulates doubt. Doubt forces us to inquire, search and deepen our understanding of issues. This exploration changes the way we understand the problems in our work.

Yet for many people ambiguity is about stress. It's the 'not knowing' that creates their anxieties. So what can they do to reduce the stress that can accompany ambiguity?

■ **Accept ambiguity as one component of a leader's life.** A huge step psychologically. It's not your job to know everything.

■ **Get into the habit of planning and thinking ahead.** You can't anticipate every contingency, but a little planning and thinking throws up 'the usual suspects' you'll need to be aware of.

■ **Know that perfection is rare.** We all make mistakes from time to time. Studies show that even the best managers only make the correct decision 65% of the time.

■ **Trust and delegate.** A tendency for many leaders is, once stress kicks in, they're on the backs of their staff checking every move. It will hurt, but let go. Trust your people to deliver.

■ **Don't expect to complete one task before moving on to another.** Leadership is just not like that. Make a significant move forward with one task and then switch to the activity you next need to focus on.

■ **Don't get caught up in the small stuff.** You have priorities. Make sure that these receive your main focus. Don't get sidetracked by low priority issues.

You must accept ambiguity as an essential factor in any leadership role.

5.8

Innovate for a great Plan B

In every change process you expect the unexpected. The roadblock that suddenly appears and you have to find a way around. Sometimes orthodox thinking gets you past it. But there are occasions when you need new thinking. An innovative solution that makes for a great Plan B.

What is the difference between creativity and innovation? Arnold Wasserman, chairman of the Idea Factory, described innovation as "…taking creative ideas and bringing them into the world". Creativity is the inventive part. Innovation is applying the creativity practically to the real world. So how do you do it? Well, there are concepts that you've probably already used like brainstorming and mind mapping. But let me share a great idea-generation tool to help your team think of innovative ways around any roadblock. It's an acronym called SCAMPER.

"The most successful people are those who are good at Plan B"

James Yorke, American mathematician

First define – in a statement – what it is that you want to solve. Then use SCAMPER to look at the roadblock in different ways.

■ **S = Substitute.** What might we substitute in place of our original plan? Think of who else, what else, other methodologies or a different approach.

■ **C = Combine.** What could we combine this with? A different blend, assortment or ensemble. What two – or more – things might we put together?

■ **A = Adapt.** What can we change to solve the problem? Do differently? What else is similar, have we done this before? Is there something we could copy?

■ **M = Modify, magnify, minify.** Can the roadblock be made smaller? Can we increase something to overcome it? What attributes could be enhanced or diminished?

■ **P = Put to other uses.** What do we already have that could be used in a different way? Is there something we could use for different purposes? Can we use something in another context?

■ **E = Eliminate.** What could we get rid of? Can you leave something out? Condense or concentrate it? Remove something?

■ **R = Rearrange or reverse.** What might we move around or mix up? Can we reverse elements? Even turn something upside down? Why don't we change our perspective or the timing?

Take a letter from the list and use it as a trigger to ask yourself questions. Capture the thoughts generated and see which ideas can help you negotiate the roadblock most successfully.

Innovation is applying a creative solution in a practical way.

Leadership influence

Great influencers understand the political landscape of an organization. If you can too, everything that follows is much easier. Build up relationships of trust with key people, offering your assistance when appropriate. You can then expect favours in return. To get to know these influencers and become one yourself, you must be good at networking. Influencing naturally involves communication, and the chapter ends with tips on presentations and on clear, concise writing.

6.1

Get wise to the politics

Why is it some leaders perform all their functions well, yet make little impact in their organization? One of the reasons is that they lack 'political savvy' and don't appreciate the underlying informal power dynamics that influence the success of key initiatives.

So what is it that people who have this 'savvy' do? Well, they know what they can and can't control. They know when to take action. Who is with them and who will be against them. They're good at influencing others to be on 'their team'. In short, they have a detailed map of the organization's political territory and where everyone sits in it.

But are we saying that you must 'schmooze' to get ahead? Definitely not. But you'll need to recognize there are forces at work in your organization that are going to influence the impact your work has. So follow these six savvy tips to get politically tuned in.

1 **Be yourself.** Earlier you'll have read about the power of being your authentic self. Demonstrate integrity, courage and trust. Such authenticity draws others to you.

one minute wonder Who are the key players in your organization that have the real power? How well do you know them? In what way could you harness their influence? What is their opinion of you and your work?

2 **Network with all in your circle of influence.** Build strong relationships with those around you. Be generous with your time and expertise.

3 **Control your verbal responses.** When is the right moment to talk about this subject? What's the best way to present the subject to keep everyone with you?

4 **Communicate upwards with the same skill you communicate down.** Recognize that your boss and your boss's boss are big influencers in what you can achieve. But don't make it an all-consuming passion.

5 **Get skilled at influencing.** Notice what works and what doesn't with individuals. Choose your timing when you need to make something happen. Build rapport with those important to your work.

6 **Observe others.** Take a step back and see what upsets certain influencers. What leaves them cold? What excites them? Understand the interactions that occur when influencers gather.

Understand the political levers that exist in your organization and the people who pull them.

6.2

Influence: open an account today!

As you come to understand a company's underlying political dynamics, you will appreciate the possibility of engaging influential people to help you achieve your goals. But how do we influence them when we have no authority?

Here are six great techniques for creating influence with others.

1 **Be clear about what you want.** You're going to be communicating your goals to others you believe can help. What they'll want is a clear message of how they can help in these goals.

2 **Open 'emotional bank accounts' with colleagues.** This is a 'trust account' which you both put into. Each makes 'deposits' with gestures such as assistance or advice. Make sure you're creditworthy before making withdrawals!

3 **Regularly interact with the people you're going to influence.** Before you influence anybody you're going to have to do some groundwork. Build the relationship first before you ask for their support with issues.

4 **Use 'pull' influencing behaviours.** 'Pull' influence is motivating others to want to help. For example, by showing how your initiative's benefits will also have positive outcomes for them.

5 **Understand others' objectives and long-term goals.** Everyone has a purpose they're working towards. Research that purpose. Show how it overlaps with your purpose. Now you'll have a better chance of getting them 'on board'.

6 **Look for the 'win-win'.** People are more receptive to others' influence when care had been taken to consider their 'win'. Your research should have already established what a 'win' situation would be for them.

If there are people who are senior to you then it's important you don't treat them as gods. They are part – as you are part – of an organizational effort to create real value. Think of them as 'partners' in your efforts. This will stop you putting them on a pedestal and asking for their 'permission' to back your projects.

Opening emotional bank accounts with key people is vital for exerting greater influence.

6.3

Give to gain when you network

Salespeople will always tell you that buyers don't buy your company, they buy you. You are your company, your department and your team. You are a figure-head that can make links with others and establish a network of expertise and contacts that make your team's working life easier. So let's look at the skills required to be an effective networker.

The two most important skills when networking are the ability to listen attentively and ask questions. You'll notice I haven't said 'talking'. When we're talking we're not learning.

case study I used to work for one of the best networkers I've ever known. Charles showed me the value networking has to a leader. One of my favourite memories involved a 2-hour delay in India's Kolkata Airport. Unperturbed, Charles fell to talking to one of the other frustrated passengers. They exchanged some anecdotes, information and business cards. I thought

So let's look at some networking tips.

■ **First, set yourself a networking goal.** For example, by the end of this conference I'm going to have the business cards of five people I'd like to have as part of my network.

■ **Build trust.** People always weigh you up when they first meet you. Make sure the impression you leave is one of someone who is positive, trustworthy and able to bring business insight.

■ **Ask more questions than you answer.** Make sure you find out as much as you can from each person. Uncover opportunity.

■ **Always stay positive.** If someone makes a negative comment always deflect it. You never know who is listening or where your negative response might end up.

■ **Be generous.** Let's say that something comes up in conversation that you've some information on. Then offer to send it to them. Whatever the gesture, look to strengthen the contact.

■ **Always introduce yourself to anyone who is on their own.** They'll be glad to talk and, if it's hard going for you, you can soon make your apologies and leave.

A rule of building great networks is that 'givers gain'.

no more about it, but a few months later the project we were engaged on ran into a roadblock in relation to Indian corporate law. Charles went straight to his PC and sent off an email requesting a clarification of our legal position. Within a day, back came the answer he needed... from the passenger he had spoken to months before in Kolkata Airport!

6.4

Negotiate so everyone wins

Everyone negotiates. From senior executives to children bargaining with their parents. Negotiation is not about 'cards up sleeves' or walking away with everything you wanted. You always have to consider the other side. Especially if it's a relationship you need to nurture.

Negotiation should involve the exchange of one valuable resource for another, so both parties achieve a satisfactory 'win-win' outcome. There are five negotiation stages:

1 **Planning.** Decide what you'd be very happy to achieve. What you'll probably achieve. What is the very least you'll accept. Be clear about these before you negotiate.

> **case study** I occasionally come up against poor negotiators. One was Steve, the sales director of a hotel chain. He used the same opening tactic every time: "Michael, you know I can't justify last year's rates in this climate so I'll need you to be reasonable. 'Reasonable' to Steve was code for 'drop your rates'.

2 **Proposal.** This is where both sides state their case. Remember that the impression you make at this stage will influence the perception the other side has of you.

3 **Debate.** Here the two sides explore the merits of the other's proposals. Experienced negotiators approach this with a shared 'problem solving' approach.

4 **Bargaining.** Usually both sides have to make concessions to reach agreement. As you 'trade', you should never concede something of great value for something which has little value.

5 **Closing.** A negotiation has been agreed and now both parties confirm what that agreement is. Commitments are made and the next stage decided.

All negotiators have a BATNA. This stands for 'Best Alternative To a Negotiated Agreement'. Deciding your BATNA or 'walk-away' is not always easy. But having an alternative path to pursue should the negotiation break down is important. It means that you don't have everything invested in the negotiation itself. This gives you greater power in the exchange.

Planning is the most crucial stage of any negotiation.

'This climate' was also meaningless. Regardless of whether it was a good or bad year, he always implied business was poor. This tactic irritated me and meant that we were never going to negotiate in an open and honest way. 'Win-lose' negotiators like Steve seldom enjoy long-term business relationships with others.

6.5

Listen to learn

Surely we don't need to talk about listening? We do it all the time! Research in 1998 found that the average individual spends between 42–60% of daily communication time listening. But they can forget, ignore, or misunderstand up to 75% of what they hear. That's a worrying statistic for any leader.

When a leader has issues with communication, I always start by working on their listening skills. When you improve their listening, other aspects of their communication often improve as well.

■ **Listen attentively.** Listening attentively is such a motivating trait in a leader. It demonstrates that what the employee is saying is of worth. Of course, when it comes to the leader speaking, such attentiveness will have encouraged the employee to reciprocate that behaviour.

■ **Know the 'Law of Listening'.** What is it we're listening for? I love the 'Law of Listening' that states, "The test for listening is learning." Many people don't listen. What they're really doing is just confirming information they already know. When a person says something they disagree with, they stop listening because the person doesn't know what they're talking about!

"Know how to listen, and you will profit even from those who talk badly" **Plutarch, Ancient Greek historian and philosopher**

■ **Listen for feelings.** Great listeners don't just listen to what's being said. They listen for feelings as well. Emotions are often more important than words. They represent the real core of a message. Words are often just a thin layer of meaning that sits on top.

■ **Enforce silence on yourself.** How do you become a better listener? Well one piece of research recommends you impose a period of silence on yourself. This really concentrates your attention on what is going on around you. You'll be staggered at how much you start to really hear.

■ **Always reserve judgment.** When someone says something you really disagree with, say to yourself, "I totally disagree with what this person is saying. What a great opportunity to learn."

■ **Ask questions.** Asking questions related to what the other speaker is saying is proof that you're listening attentively. Just looking at them while they're speaking is not listening. They will soon tell if you've 'switched off'.

If we only listen to things we know already then our learning will never grow. Only when our thinking is challenged do we open ourselves up to real learning. Listening helps us achieve that.

Don't switch off because you disagree with something the other speaker says.

6.6

Prepare to present

One of the 'must-have' requirements of any leader is to speak in front of others – often using PowerPoint or some other visual aid. Not everyone is equally comfortable with this. But don't despair. If it's not one of your strengths then let me share these ten great presentation tips with you.

1 **Prepare thoroughly.** Brainstorm or mind-map your presentation. Write each topic and sub-topic on a separate post-it note. Arrange these along a timeline in the order of the presentation.

2 **Practise!** Run through the entire presentation twice. Rehearse the opening five minutes repeatedly until it's perfect. A great opening will build confidence.

3 **Get them listening from the outset.** Tell them a funny story (make sure it is funny) or an astonishing statistic.

4 **Relax.** If you get nervous try and keep still, but walk around if it makes you feel more relaxed. People will relax with you.

5 **Don't fiddle.** Don't fiddle nervously with a pen or other object during the presentation. Use your hands for expressing yourself. Otherwise have them lightly clasped in front of you.

6 **Be enthusiastic.** A passionate, enthusiastic speaker can make every mistake in the book and still be listened to attentively by their audience. Be enthusiastic and they'll hear every word!

7 **Don't overuse PowerPoint.** Used in moderation PowerPoint is a useful visual tool. But be prepared to use other media as well – or even none at all!

8 **Involve the audience.** Ask for comments about slides. Stimulate short discussions. Try and punctuate your presentation with opportunities for others to contribute.

9 **Make sure your 'call to action' is last.** If you want people to make a commitment, then make sure it's in your last slides. People often easily recall the closing points of a presentation.

10 **Deal with questions.** If you don't know the answer, say so and get back to the questioner. Or ask the audience for their thoughts first and then add your own answer.

Practice takes the pain out of presenting.

6.7

Write as you lead

My old English teacher, Mr. Culligan, was a great man. "As you speak, so you write," he'd say. And he was right. Now I have a saying of my own, "As you write, so you lead." The way any written communication is crafted conveys something of your style of leadership. It will speak through your words.

It's no use being courageous, ambitious and interpersonally brilliant if you contradict it with emails that are sloppy, disjointed and grammatically incorrect. Leaders have to master every form of written communication. They must remember all types of communication can have a real impact on their people.

When do we use written communication? Examples that come to mind are electronic bulletin boards, emails, personal notes, presentation slides, margin notes in reports and appraisal documents. All, in their own way, are permanent records and need to be carefully prepared.

So let's agree some rules for good written communication.

■ **Use vocabulary that everyone understands.** Avoid highly technical or complicated words. Writing in simple language is a skill. For example, "I am cognizant..." is better written as "I am aware..."

"Four basic premises of writing: clarity, brevity, simplicity and humanity" **William Zinsser, American writer and editor**

■ **Never trust a spell checker.** While writing this book, I typed the word "besides", or so I thought. The spell checker saw nothing wrong with what I had actually typed, which was "bedsides".

■ **Avoid slang.** You may understand its meaning but will your reader?

■ **Don't use idioms.** Idioms don't translate and suggest a degree of informality that might be inappropriate.

■ **Only use abbreviations the reader will understand.** Everyone might know 'USA' but struggle with a more obscure abbreviation. If you're going to use abbreviations then explain them in brackets the first time they appear.

■ **Spell people's names correctly.** It's embarrassing to write "Mark's a key player" and then discover his name is 'Marc'. It shows a real lack of attention to detail.

■ **Write short sentences.** This will ensure that people understand your meaning. Long sentences are more confusing and cloud meaning.

Another consideration is that staff reading your written communications may not have your first language as their first language. In this situation you have to be even more careful about how you write.

Your written communication reveals a lot about you, so deserves special care.

109   Leadership **secrets**

Leadership
and the
team

The best leader is one whose team chooses to follow. To be a successful leader you need a great team around you. But the team has to be dynamic, focused and able to deliver. This chapter explains how you create the right environment for them to take on new responsibility. It also shows how to lead in this age of virtual teams and teleconferencing.

7.1

Build an empowered team

Trends come and go. But somehow the word 'empowerment' never seems to go away. I believe it's because, when you look behind the trendy word, there is some substance. But first let's do away with the idea that you 'empower people'. I believe you create the conditions for people to feel empowered.

Out there you'll find many attempts to define empowerment. I see it as building a team's ability and belief that they can make decisions that impact the organization they work in. These aren't small decisions like changing the style of paper clip that's used. They're decisions about the 'big stuff' the team is part of.

But making a team feel empowered is not going to happen overnight. It's a 'long game' you're going to have to play. So let's look at how you recognize an empowered team.

■ **They have the power to make decisions.** This hurts the micromanager, who sees it as 'organizational suicide'. But if you're serious about empowerment then you have to introduce a level of independence.

"The function of leadership is to produce more leaders, not more followers" Ralph Nader, American attorney and activist

■ **They have access to information.** If you want decisions to be good decisions, then that involves the team having access to all the information they need.

■ **They have access to resources.** A big failing of many empowerment initiatives is that they never give the necessary resources to support the process. Resources could be people, money, facilities, etc.

■ **They are fired by an inner belief that they make a difference.** Disempowered teams believe they can't change anything. Empowered teams have a genuine conviction that they can really make a positive impact.

■ **They have a sense of accountability.** They are answerable for their decisions. If the leader 'takes the blame' then real accountability was never given to the team in the first place.

■ **They are self-organizing.** The team members have to demonstrate the ability to work together, organize their own workload and arrange resources by themselves.

Getting a team to this stage is a big achievement for a leader. Keeping them there is another thing. One action that will certainly help you is praising the good decisions they make. Failing to do this, or only mentioning the occasions when they get it wrong, will soon puncture the empowerment balloon.

An empowered team makes decisions that have real impact on the success of the organization.

7.2

Stretch that team!

The world is full of team motivation theories. Many are interesting but difficult to apply in the day-to-day activity of working life. So let's have a motivation theory-free discussion about how to stretch your team. What can we do to maintain a strong internal desire for achievement?

Successful teams are those that function at a high level of capability. Knowing you're part of a great team is pretty inspiring in itself. Because you're leading a group of highly capable individuals you have to continue to excite and inspire them towards new challenges. It keeps that sense of motivation at the level you want. Here are some tips to keep it growing!

case study One organization I work with knows that using employees to recruit is a real motivator. Not only does the person on reception have a say, but also the actual team the candidate will work with. The reception administrator assesses their values. She makes polite conversation. Then assesses how receptive and friendly they were. Some candidates, she says, reserve

"Never tell people how to do things. Tell them what to do and they will surprise you with their ingenuity"

George Patton, US General

■ **Surprise people with real challenges.** Take them aside and hand over meaningful, interesting work. It breaks the day-to-day routine and fires people up with the prospect of an interesting assignment.

■ **Use stretch goals.** Some people don't always realize what they're really capable of. Where you believe someone can really work towards a 'stretch goal' then make it happen.

■ **Get to know what motivates each individual.** Sounds obvious? Some leaders don't do it. Everyone has different motivators – find out what they are and lead with these motivators in mind.

■ **Bring them into your world.** Show them what your issues are. The angle from which you're looking at problems. Introduce a leadership viewpoint.

■ **Get people deeply involved.** Superficial responsibility seldom motivates anyone. But having a deep commitment and involvement in something can be very motivating.

Challenge people and get them deeply involved in the work they do.

their friendliness for the interview panel. Now they've learned something important about their attitude to people! After the interview, the team chat with the candidate. They find out a great deal because the candidate often believes the interview is over. The success of this recruitment method is reflected in an impressive employee retention rate.

7.3

Upset your team's thinking

As a leader, it's vital that your team doesn't begin to 'groupthink'. This is where a team's strong sense of cohesion and camaraderie starts to take away their objectivity. Rather than be seen to 'rock the boat' in meetings, they feel they should preserve the team's sense of togetherness.

Here are some of the signs that will help you spot when your team is suffering from 'groupthink':

■ They don't consider the full range of alternatives available to them when assessing an issue.

one minute wonder Has 'groupthink' ever infected a team you've been part of? What decisions were weaker because this occurred? When did the team start to fall into this trap? What can you do so that your team doesn't begin to conform in this way?

■ Once they've chosen a possible solution, they don't examine it thoroughly to test its strengths and weaknesses.

■ If they've rejected an alternative once, they won't reconsider it in the light of new information. "We've tried that before."

■ They don't objectively research options. They might only collect evidence that reflects their biased choice.

■ They never consider contingency plans.

But don't despair! Here are some helpful techniques to make sure this doesn't happen.

■ **Tell the team what 'groupthink' is.** It's a great way of raising awareness to it. Most people hate to think this is what they might be doing.

■ **Use a 'rotating chair' to lead the meetings.** Don't always chair the meeting yourself. Have other people take turns to chair it. It changes the dynamic and shifts the emphasis of power in the team.

■ **Consider the outside view.** Do you know anyone who has an external view on what's being discussed? Invite them in to make a challenging presentation to the team.

■ **Don't let the team know your viewpoint.** This sometimes channels the team's thinking. Withhold your view and see what others really believe.

■ **Play devil's advocate.** Either you can do this or get someone to take the role on. Challenge the received wisdom. Ask people to justify their thinking. Argue against the point from different angles.

■ **Get people to consult and report back.** This isn't always possible if you're under time pressure. However, it takes people outside the group and allows them to explore other viewpoints.

Challenge your team's traditional ways of doing things to prevent them from falling into the trap of 'groupthink'.

7.4

Mentor your leaders-in-waiting

My challenge to leaders is to ask who they are currently developing to take over from them. People aren't born ready for leadership. Even if they have all the skills talked about in this book, they're still going to need to be prepared for leadership. Mentoring is one of the most effective techniques you can use.

People have different needs from a mentor. Some want an 'expert' to help them with the technical stuff. Some want someone they can 'bounce ideas around with'. Find out what type of mentor your 'leader-in-waiting' would like.

Leadership is often a lonely role. It's not always possible to turn to others for advice. So they need to prepare to be able to operate independently. Your role in this? Well, you're now a leader and the journey has taught you a lot. Surely all you do now is impart the sum total of your wisdom?

Hold on there! Doing this isn't going to develop a leader. They're not going to meet exactly the same issues you did. So you can't give them a neat leadership manual. But you can develop something much more valuable: their ability to think for themselves.

"Mentor: someone whose hindsight can become your foresight" **Anonymous**

You're going to have to get their thinking 'muscle' tuned up. And like any other muscle, if they don't use it they might lose it. So make sure you never do their thinking for them. Get them to begin to think for themselves. As their mentor, be reluctant just to answer their questions. Remember the purpose is to get them to think independently.

■ "I'm not sure how to deal with this new marketing director. He's so rude." "You've got to assert yourself, Nikki. Show him you're no pushover." Wrong! You've just disengaged Nikki's thinking muscle. Let's try that again.

■ "I'm not sure how to deal with this new marketing director. He's so rude." "What does he do that makes you feel that way, Nikki?" Now we can explore the director's behaviour. Why he does it. And then ask Nikki to think about what she could do to deal with the situation.

Mentoring can be about advice. But when you're grooming a leader, you need to make sure you're developing their skills. Not just showing off your own.

To mentor a future leader, develop their ability to think for themselves.

7.5

Trust the virtual team

Some organizations have abandoned the traditional hierarchy. But if that wasn't complex enough, they've often added a second layer of difficulty for leaders: creating virtual teams with team members located at different places all around the world. Here are nine tips to help you successfully lead your virtual team.

1 **Start with everyone in one room.** Getting them to meet first in person really alters the way people feel about each other.

2 **Begin with some ground rules.** Get people to sign up to some basic courtesies for working together. Establish rules about contributing, disagreeing and the general 'codes of behaviour' people should expect.

3 **Ensure that you deal with everyone equally.** Some people who are co-located with the leader can often get more favourable treatment. Make sure this doesn't happen.

4 **Get to know individuals outside the team meetings.** Make sure you have one-to-ones with all the team members. Just the same way you'd do if they sat in the office with you.

5 **Provide relevant and timely feedback to all members.** Don't forget to give equal amounts of feedback to everyone. Don't have any employee working in a 'feedback vacuum'.

6 **Consider time zones.** If you want a full contribution then don't arrange meetings when key members should be asleep. You'll probably find they soon are!

7 **Understand the cultures of those you're working with.** Get to know some of the 'codes of conduct' that operate in their cultures. Remember, for example, that in some parts of the world "Yes" doesn't always mean "Yes".

8 **Think about what you say.** Try and make sure that your words can't be misrepresented or even taken too literally. Avoid local sayings and idiomatic expressions.

9 **Be consistent in your rewards and recognition.** Again, avoid favouring certain individuals over others.

As a leader, you're expected to be technically able and have the usual project management skills. You must also set standards for how people should communicate and interact with each other.

Give equal weight to the needs of all the members of the team.

7.6

Inject life into your teleconference

Chairing a meeting with everyone in the room is difficult enough. But running a meeting when participants are dialling in from all over the globe is a real challenge! Many leaders now use teleconferencing because of the great advantages it brings. But they're only advantages when the leader uses these ten important teleconferencing techniques.

1   **Use your voice effectively.** Make sure you vary the pitch. A boring voice can soon have everyone yawning and losing interest.

2   **Follow the normal rules of conducting a meeting.** It's what you would expect from any competent chairperson. Keep to the agenda and control unwanted interruptions. Keep enthusiasm high and make sure people are contributing.

3   **Introduce yourself and the meeting purpose.** You set the tone of the teleconference when you do this. Make sure it's prepared, enthusiastic and not overlong.

4 **Ensure everyone introduces themselves at the start.** Introduce yourself first, then ask others to do the same.

5 **Remind everyone of the ground rules.** These should have been decided at the first meeting. Go through them so everyone's aware of how they will ensure an effective teleconference.

6 **Don't allow one speaker to dominate.** If someone's presenting a lot of information, then ask for comments occasionally so people have a break from listening to just one voice.

7 **Use names to bring people in.** Invite people with phrases such as "Ekon in Abuja, how does this affect…"

8 **Keep it democratic.** Make a note of which people and sites are contributing. Invite comments from those who haven't spoken yet.

9 **Stick to the timescale.** People often have other meetings scheduled after yours. Respect this. Use the time pressure to keep participants' contributions concise and to the point.

10 **Close the teleconference professionally.** Summarize what's been agreed and recap action items. Ask participants for suggestions as to how the next teleconference could be improved.

One common mistake is trying to cover too much on a teleconference. It is far better to cover three to five points thoroughly rather than cover more items superficially.

Keep the conference lively and try to get everyone to participate.

Jargon buster

Bargaining

In negotiation, the exchange of one item of value for another of equal worth.

Big picture

The complete perspective on a situation or issue.

Brainstorming

A high-energy method of getting people to suggest ideas and actions before critically assessing their worth.

Change curve

The stages employees go through when they experience change in their lives.

Collaboration

In management, collaboration is defined as working together (often with someone outside the team) to achieve a goal and secure a business benefit.

Comfort zone

At work, an environment in which someone can carry out their tasks without risk of being challenged. A mental or physical boundary someone stays within.

Competence

The ability to do something well. Carrying out a task to the necessary standard.

Culture

Usually thought of as the general customs and beliefs of a group of people.

Devil's advocate

Someone arguing against a certain position. They are not committed to their side of the argument but take on the role only to test the validity of a position.

Flag-carrier

An employee who willingly disseminates and demonstrates a key strategic message or behaviour to others in a team.

Matrix organization

A business structure that has both horizontal and vertical lines of authority. Often matrix employees might have two or more people to report to.

Micromanager

A manager who has no trust in their employees and so closely oversees every small action and activity.

Mind-mapping

A diagram which organizes tasks, ideas or words grouped around a central key word or idea. Developed by Tony Buzan and widely used around the world.

Motivation

The enthusiasm that someone has for carrying out a task or responsibility. Also the reason or need for making sure a task is carried out.

Networking

The practice of establishing mutually beneficial relationships with other people who are usually often outside their immediate circle of contacts.

Open-door policy

The behaviour of a manager that encourages their staff to feel free to approach them at any time to discuss important matters.

Paint pictures

The translation of concepts into a visual image so that people retain the core message more easily. For example the conveying of difficult business conditions as 'stormy weather'.

Political savvy

A shrewd insight into the dynamics of an organization that helps an individual achieve their goals. Often a set of unwritten rules about working successfully within a structure.

Rework

To return to a completed task and improve it so that it meets a higher standard.

Rotating chair

The practice of allowing each team member – in turn – to chair a meeting rather than the team's leader.

Stakeholder

An individual who is directly or indirectly affected by an action, policy or objective.

Strategy

A detailed plan for successfully achieving an agreed goal. Often based on: Where am I now? Where do I want to get to? How will I get there?

Top-line theme

The main message that you want people to retain. The term originally derived from the fact that overall revenues appear at the top of an income statement.

Tough call

A difficult decision that has to be made usually between two equally unattractive alternatives.

Work-life balance

The prioritizing of the demands of both one's work and personal life so that each receives the necessary attention.

Further reading

As well as recommending the following books I also have a number of articles and in-house management and employee workshops available at www.mhconsult.com

Adair, John *John Adair's 100 Greatest Ideas for Effective Leadership and Management* (Capstone, 2002) ISBN 978-1841121406

Back, Ken and Kate *Assertiveness at Work* (McGraw Hill, 1999) ISBN 978-0077114282

Bennis, Warren G. and Nanus, Bert *Leadership: Strategies for Taking Charge* (Harper Business Essentials, 2003) ISBN 978-0060913366

Bossidy, Larry and Charan, Ram *Execution: The Discipline of Getting Things Done* (Random House Business Books, 2002) ISBN 978-0712625982

Chhokar, Jagdeep S., Brodbeck, Felix C. and House, Robert J. *Culture and Leadership Across the World: The GLOBE Book of In-depth Studies of 25 Societies* (Psychology Press, 2007) ISBN 978-0805859973

Connolly, Mickey and Rianoshek, Richard *The Communication Catalyst* (Kaplan, 2002) ISBN 978-0793149049

Connors, Roger, Hickman, Craig R, and Smith, Tom *The Oz Principle: Getting Results Through Individual and Organizational Accountability* (Portfolio, 2004) ISBN 978-1591840244

Covey, Stephen R. *7 Habits of Highly Effective People: Powerful Lessons in Personal Change* (Simon and Schuster, 2004) ISBN 978-0743272452

Deschamps, Jean-Philippe *Innovation Leaders: How Senior Executives Stimulate, Steer and Sustain Innovation* (John Wiley and Sons, 2008) ISBN 978-0470515242

Fisher, Kimball and Mareen *The Distance Manager: A Hands on Guide to Managing Off-Site Employees and Virtual Teams* (McGraw-Hill Professional, 2000) ISBN 978-0071360654

Fisher, R. and Ury, W. *Getting to Yes* (Penguin Books, 2008) ISBN 978-1844131464

Goleman, Daniel *Working with Emotional Intelligence* (Bloomsbury, 1999) ISBN 978-0747543848

Harvard Business School *Harvard Business Essentials: Strategy* (Harvard Business School, 2005) ISBN 978-1591396321

Lencioni, Patrick *The Five Dysfunctions of a Team* (Jossey-Bass, 2002) ISBN 978-0787960759

McGregor, Douglas *Leadership and Motivation* (MIT Press, 1966) ISBN 978-0262130233

Michaelson, Gerald A. *Sun Tzu: The Art of War for Managers – 50 Strategic Rules* (Adams Media, 2001) ISBN 978-1580624596

Nelson, Robert B. *Empowering Employees through Delegation* (Longman Higher Education, 1994) ISBN 978-0786301997

Pincus, Marilyn *Managing Difficult People: A Survival Guide for Handling Any Employee* (Adams Media, 2005) ISBN 978-1593371869

Porter, Michael E. *Competitive Strategy: Techniques for Analyzing Industries and Competitors* (Free Press, 2004) ISBN 978-0743260886

Semler, Ricardo *Maverick!: The Success Story Behind the World's Most Unusual Workplace* (Random House Business Books, 2001) ISBN 978-0712678865

Senge, Peter M. *The Fifth Discipline: The Art and Practice of the Learning Organization* (Random House Business Books, 2006) ISBN 978-0712656870

Tate, Rick and White, Julie *People Leave Managers...Not Organizations* (iUniverse Books, 2005) ISBN 978-0595779765

Tavris, Carol and Aronson, Elliot *Mistakes Were Made (but Not by Me)* (Pinter and Martin, 2008) ISBN 978-1905177219

Whitmore, John *Coaching for Performance* (Nicholas Brealey Publishing, 2002) ISBN 978-1857885354

Wiseman, Richard *The Luck Factor: The Scientific Study of the Lucky Mind* (Arrow, 2004) ISBN 978-0099443247

www.BusinessSecrets.net